WHERE MY HEART IS

COLLECTED POEMS

BY ANDRE N. VAN CHAU

Copyright

ERIN GO BRAGH Publishing

www.ErinGoBraghPublishing.com

CONTENTS

THE RIVERS

My thought meanders, over mossy rocks:
The river started with a drop of water,
became a trickle,
lost again and again
under dead leaves and dried branches,
stopped in greenish pools
that reflected long-legged spiders.
The mountain stream had no name,
not knowing where and when it would meet the sea,
not knowing the immense power of its drops of water!

My thought knows where it goes
aware of its power, loving and fearing its end.
My being shaped by my thought.
and my thought
Is and is not a river.
It flies over river bends,
Stops and listens to the whisper, and the roars, and the rumble
Of the river water.

When the river plunges into the sea
losing its identity in white foam or turbid waves
my thought still hovers high in the white clouds.
With unbroken wings, it challenges the winds of changes
it knows -- without proof -- horizons far away
Over the sea.
It knows it's not alone.
It senses thoughts of millions of its brothers and sisters
hovering high in the white clouds.

My fate is invisibly bound to other fates
My end comes and joins other ends.
O river! Be you the smallest stream without name

Snaking through bamboo jungles
Or the all-powerful Huang He
casting and recasting the fates of a billion lives,
no matter,
you led my thought on the first days of its flight
then you let it go, free like the wind
like a white cloud
in the luminous sky.

When finally you merge with other rivers
in the immensity of the sea,
my thought enters the universe of thoughts
where human minds, and human fates
of all humanity, past, present and future
fuse in a sky of fire
A fire that burns
until
only love remains.
Until only love remains.

THE KILLING OF A DREAM

The little girl in a dirty red polka dot dress
sat for hours in the grass
watching a wounded butterfly
that tried to mend its tattered wings.

"What do you do there, little girl?" I asked,
not really wanting to know;
"--- I am healing the poor butterfly with my eyes," she said.
The little girl in the dirty red polka dot dress
had beautiful, large hazel eyes.
"--- You are crazy, my little girl! Your eyes cannot heal!"
There were tears welling in her eyes:
"--- I am healing the poor butterfly with my eyes and my prayer",
she screamed.
"---Seen any result? Crazy girl!" I said.
I walked away – not looking back
knowing I had killed
maybe the first dream of the little girl.

She would have other dreams, of course.
but there are other adults like me
to kill them too.
One by one, all her dreams small and big
until there are no more dreams
nor tears, nor prayer, in her large hazel eyes.

MY LITTLE CANYON

I live at Steiner Ranch,
In the hilly city of Austin, Texas,
my house is built on the cliff of a canyon.
Not mine the live oaks twisted like giant bonsai trees
clamping their gnarled roots around unyielding limestones
not mine the mansions hiding behind tall walls on the hilltop,
my little canyon with a trickle
of water enough to invite cottonmouths
or harmless water snakes alike.
Who cares if they are venomous or not, I don't.
The little school of silvery fish
swimming innocently and leisurely
until snapped by the snakes
don't care to dispute their fate!
I walk on slippery moss
on round stones
and half immersed gravel
enjoying sunbeam piercing through live oak leaves
The little canyon between two vertiginous white cliffs
The mighty -- because patient -- trickle of water
plus weight of time
has made its existence possible.
Sometimes looking up from the little canyon
I wonder:
what Herculean tasks would I accomplish
if my years were much longer
Like the men and women in Genesis?
Looking up from the bottom of my little canyon
the sky I see is a blue silk scarf
no more than a blue silk scarf:
So many men and women, like little frogs
looking up from small dark pits
Never stop
wondering why the sky is so small.

DARK LABYRINTH

It was a dark winter night
I walked in long strides in a strange city
that throbbed like a prodded heart,
pumping its fear and anger into the night.

The streets were forbidding
walled with shadows
and slippery like slow-moving monstrous snakes
"Keep walking and don't look down",
I told myself.
"How many have you killed?",
the voice asked.

"I have killed no one, if I remember well", I said.
I walked on as if the question were not insulting
nor insisting enough to deserve a reply.

"How many times have you killed yourself?"
the voice whispered.
"I don't know. And I don't care",
I said, but remembering a score of times
I have done more than killing myself.

Why on a tenebrous night
any question could be asked?
I wondered.
Walking alone in that unfamiliar city
of an alien land,
in a far-off continent,
I guessed I was lost
and was indeed lost
*

In a veil of mist
That my numbed fingers were unable to part.
I walked on, surrounded by
barely visible ghosts
who did not appear threatening
who were not trying to scare
and who were just sullen and sad .

The greatest danger
when you walk
in an unfamiliar city at night
is the fusion of past
and present:
ghosts of the past
walk with you, a multitude of them
bent down with shame and guilt
none of them proud
and never smiling
(having no lips)
They may laugh, but their laughs are hollow
cavernous and halting.

How to deal with sorrowful ghosts walking around you?
Yet you know how well you have managed your life:
(yes, you have managed it quite well)
Doesn't *that* count for something?
The past with its profound sadness
Says: "No".

Your thoughts go in circles
slowly, very slowly, like the cycles of seasons
Springs, summers, autumns and winters;
like the birth, growth, and decline
of empires;

like cooling planets circling around a dying sun
with no purpose;
like a tired runner trapped in a labyrinth
finding no exit;
like a poor disconsolate soul
trying to escape
its cycle of reincarnation.

You cannot run faster than your familiar ghosts!
you cannot build a nest with your broken dreams;
you will know sooner or later
that hell and heaven, nirvana and nothingness
are the same.

For the moment, be content with your purposeless pilgrimage:
As you touch the walls of your labyrinth
Oozing blood, sweat and tears
You understand your fate.

and yet you have to hope
even if hope is all you have;
you have to love
even if love doesn't conquer all;
you have to keep walking
even if you are in a labyrinth.
That's your fate!

I found that inhuman truth one cold, dark night
walking in the slippery streets
of an unfamiliar city
Long ago.

I found that wisdom
while I was lost
in the labyrinth of my mind ,

walking without a map
In a sleepy and inhospitable city
not finding the exit
out of a deadly labyrinth.

I walked with my head bent low
and heard that expected but harsh sentence
handed out to me in a gust of wet and icy wind
by an invisible judge:
"The tribunal recognizes that
though you have committed no crime
against others
You did commit
multiple times murder
of the most inhuman nature
against yourself."

"You are right, your honor!"
Was my only answer.
The sentencing
Would come much later.
Again listening to the judge, or judges
I only found the penalty light
I knew others with lesser wrongdoings
Condemned to death.

So, I walked on, without a map
In an unfamiliar city
Knowing that the night would stretch
In space and time
I walked on, filled with sadness.

PILGRIMAGES

The shrine stands on the other distant shore
no boat goes there until the snow melts,
in later Spring, he learned,
and only when the ice floe on the lake
is gone.
The pilgrim stood and looked
at the frozen lake
and on the distant shore
the inaccessible shrine
shrouded in mystery.
*

Leaning on his pilgrim staff
he regretted that he had not spent time
in his past
To learn how to walk on water or on thin ice.
The shrine on the other shore
Would keep its mystery forever…

… I had known him for years:
he was the eternal pilgrim
who wandered from sacred place to sacred place,
always haunted by the insensate fear
of not having enough time
to visit all the shrines
All over the world.
*

I have always waited for him to come back
from his pilgrimages;
and have always hoped that one day
He would tell me what was driving him
to spend his life searching
in the remotest places,

for something eternally elusive,
and whether what he found there
rewarded him enough for his pain.

But every time
all he said, with a smile, was:
"Let's have another cup of jasmine tea, my friend!"
his half- closed eyes
filled with tearful visions …
Then, the next day, he was gone.
*
I somehow know that some day
in the near future,
the questions I want to ask
the answers he fails to deliver
would not matter anymore.
He will be gone one day
And never come back.

DESTINATION

The road snakes its way into the jungle.
He hesitates
not knowing
whether
he should risk being ambushed
by hundreds of blood-sucking leeches?
It rains lightly on the palms and leaves
and tangled vines of aging climbers:
The hungry leeches more ready than ever
to launch themselves like nasty projectiles
that cling on any square inch of human bare skin.

Should he risk being ambushed
by armies of noisy and hungry mosquitos
or millions of foraging marabunta ants?
he hesitates
not knowing
whether
to advance or backtrack .
The jungle in front is like any other jungle
In the tropical world,
But surely unlike the jungle inside
himself.

He has risked his life many times entering thick jungles
but has never dared enter
the jungle inside himself.

Call it introspection, call it examination of conscience,
call it self-analysis
call it soul-searching,
call it navel-gazing:

he prefers to gamble away his life
in senseless adventures
but doesn't want any part of that…
that mortal game of looking inside himself.

He may wade in turbid waters,
or venture into foggy forests, at night,
but no introspection, please!

Maybe some day
when he is old and bent and blind
and after having gone through thousands of trials
all of them left him with a bitter taste;
when his neighbors start calling him "wise",
while he knows full-well that he has been just a fool,
a plaything in the hand of a prankish fate
maybe someday,
when he realizes
there is *no hope* for him in afterlife
will he look into the darkness inside his soul,
not asking for mercy.

IN MEMORIAM

To my friend Alexis Nguyễn Văn Vĩnh

There was a time when the phone rang
my soul responded but my hand delayed;
the moment you started greeting
as the fear mounted
I did not know what horizon we would search
what depth we would go to find the beginning of a question.

I did not know how much soul searching would be involved
whether I had the strength that particular day to follow your drift.

So many questions we asked
So few answers we found!
Yet each call you made filled my day with fear and savage joy.

Now you are gone, and my line went dead,
Who will talk to me about God, and Hell, and Hell on earth?
Who will talk to me about sin and redemption?

I reread the books we read together
turning the yellowed pages.

I walk alone among the live oaks,
thinking about so much exploration,
so much pain we shared.
All I can do is to look at the people you loved
who feel the same way the emptiness around us.
All I can do is to listen to their excited litanies of the joys in time past.

But there will be an end to all this,
when the stars shine around us
when the suns and the moons revolve under our feet
among the fleecy flocks of white clouds.

And then we will renew our discussions
momentarily interrupted.

Then there will be fewer questions,
and many more answers.
there will be more light than darkness;
there will be more shine than rain.

I will stand and contemplate a beautiful soul chiseled by our Maker;
and those who loved you and missed you
will sing in unison
to the music of angels.

SCENT OF JASMINE

How suave and penetrating!
How subtle yet enduring!
those little white snow drops
half hidden under shining green leaves
Have enchanted me year after year!

Long before crude sunlight
comes and dissipates my waking dreams
wisps of heavenly scent
fuse with my half-forgotten memories
as I trample on the dewy grass
besides jasmine trellis.

Scent of jasmine
are you telling me:
"Open your heart
Let my invisible balm penetrate your soul
Cleansing it, eliminating its arrogance
and its worldliness?"

Are you saying:
"Let me soothe and heal
and guide you
toward hidden doors
that lead
to heavenly lights
and holy nothingness,
to long-desired splendor
of blessed melancholy?"

Yes, the hidden doors
that wait patiently to open on immortal bliss
or cherished sinful delight when stumbled on!
(Should I say: "no, thanks, but no."?)

*

Scent of jasmine
Suave and penetrating,
subtle yet enduring!
Should I say:
"Let me be with my blessed loneliness
or take me to
Anywhere but here!"

RAMPARTS

Against the darkening sky
your strong chiseled outline stood
resolute
how many thousand nights of my childhood and youth
you stood guard
protecting my dreams and those
of my early companions
all imperial citadel residents.

I grew up inside your walls.
your ramparts, your moats
O my imperial city!

How many dreams were woven
there
and pursued under other skies;
but it was there
that they were conceived
And born,
here within the defensive ramparts
of the imperial city!

It was here
that children holding long strings
flew their multicolored musical kites
in a cloudy sky
under the benevolent eyes of ancient Cannon-Gods.

It was here
the last dynasty was founded, declined and perished.
It was here that the last glimpses
of horses and elephants
were caught,
battle horses and battle elephants

mounted by warrior- riders
under golden parasols
bristled with long spears
on the top of the ramparts
Ages ago.

It was also within these ramparts
hundreds of my contemporaries died:
the ramparts
no longer protecting
but trapping them inside,
among a terrified crowd
of over ten thousand souls
cutting their retreat.

Over these ramparts,
the same sky now seems painted with sadness
slumbering on the narrow plain
like a dark and colossal monster
that doesn't want to be awakened
any time soon.

SOLITUDE

"Why do you abhor solitude?
Since when has it been divorced from freedom?"
"I treasure the hours spent in a quiet desert, he said
I am reborn in every wilderness
and rejoice
at opportunities to confront myself alone."
I don't understand that savage joy
of people who fall victims of their introspection.
Oh, yes, I know that ordinarily
Men are building on mudflats and wastelands
and shunning loneliness,
only find solace in crowds.
He said:
"I weep for men
who cannot face themselves
As I weep for me
who cannot face myself."
He said:
"Love your solitude,
the cradle of human thoughts,
human inventions,
and (why not?) human progress!"
"In solitude your prayer is listened to
if not by God
then by divine nature.
In solitude human wounds are healed
and lonely men and women find
pathways that may lead to unhoped-for revelation
About themselves."
He said:
"Love your solitude
little ones who run after butterflies
trampling green grass and wildflowers!
away from the embrace of your mothers,

Enjoy your moments of freedom!"
"Remember:
only in solitude you may taste
the heavenly sweetness.
of melancholy brooding."
"Little ones running on the dewy grass
may your private joy last!"
"Remember : the lonely mountain streams
are by far more inspiring than
a channeled river
crossing an urban sprawl".
He said:
"Love your solitude young men and women
brooding is not only for old folk,
meditations not only for religious,
contentment not only for the sated,
love your solitude."
But of course, I know
there are solitude and solitude:
in prison I have seen
unhappy men and women clung to prison bars,
willing to trade years of solitude
for a moment of shared privacy!
We may all dread solitude in old age
After all our loved companions are gone.
We may all dread dying in solitude
even , as he said : "solitude is full of blessed silence.
Let's love that silence in death!"
*
Yet I see the irony
of people erecting elaborate tombstones
that still try to speak
after the dead have entered the other kingdom
Where rule silence
and eternal solitude!

POETRY

Poets are shapeless clay
breathed upon and molded by divine spirit.
Poems are wordless prayers
played upon by angels' muted harps,
and sung by angels' magnificent but barely audible voices.

Poems never point directly
to a simple meaning,
(Sometimes they have no meaning at all!)
Their essence is a shining mountain
shaped like a hundred-facetted diamond
suggesting but never elaborating
fleeting images, elusive emotions,
endless joy and sadness
universe in cold fusion,
or incandescent oceans!

Man walks in the valley of tears
burdened with guilt and regrets
responds readily to the lure of poetry.

He feels unendurable pain and inhuman thirst
if poetry is taken away
even for a minute.

The hearts and minds of men
were formed in the crucible of childhood dreams,
and lullabies,
visited by mothers' smiles.

Without poetry children would grow stunted
and in many respects
unfit for life.

Without rhythms and rhymes
and poetry
Without occasional distortions of time
and poetry
Without plasticity of space
and poetry
Without the union of dreams and realities
and poetry
Men and women
even the strongest
would not have the tiniest chance of survival!

FEAR

We embrace fear for we are but humans!
The sky is too high, the sea too deep
The days too short, nights too long,
The world too large, space too expansive!

Fear preserves us in its cocoon
since our childhood.
Fear guides the baby's first steps.
It plays hide and seek with him.
As he walks and falls.

Fear is mother of all wisdom
I have never met a wise man nor a wise woman
who has not trembled
between a thought and the act.

What can we do without fear?
What can we invent
if not pushed by fear?

The fear of hunger made us plant and harvest
and store.
The fear of cold and rain and ice
made us build houses, put up roofs and weave our clothing.
The fear of wars made us built ramparts, dig moats
and design our armors
and manufacture our weapons.

The world wants us to praise fearlessness
but we know better!
The world wants us to be daring, intrepid
but we have seen how many so called heroes or adventurers
die before their allotted time.

Oh yes, let them praise fearlessness,
but let us embrace fear with gratitude
Fear, our most profound and priceless instinct!

As long as humanity exists
there will always be fear;
But if some day for good or bad reasons
fear disappears from the world
the world will soon disappear.
Mark my word!

THE SOLDIER

The soldier did not know it yet
but that was his last hour!
He listened to the rumble of cannon
and the thumping noise of mortar explosions
and the whizzing of bullets
He closed his eyes and summoned his courage
and jumped out of his foxhole
and charged the unseen enemy together
with all the men of his platoon
his automatic rifle blazing!
An enemy straddling a tree fork up high
strained his gun on him and fired .

He felt death, soothing death
before he saw his flesh
flying out of his gaping wounds
before he looked and wondered
at the weird angle his broken leg made.

His hands flew to his stomach
his blood was warm and thick
he half closed his eyes
registering the buzz of the familiar swarms of flies
of the jungle
that were about to feed on him.

But he noticed in half a second from his half closed eyes
That the enemy had withdrawn
and someone
fell from the tree.
He died knowing the mission of his platoon
was accomplished
and his death avenged.

BEAUTY

There was a time
I was in love with a tall Ming vase
I loved that light green celadon masterpiece
that was perfection!
As soon as the museum doors opened
I hurried in, found my favorite bench,
sat down and watched it for hours
mesmerized by its superhuman beauty.

There was a time
I fell in love with Bach's Cantata
O Ewigkeit, du Donnerwort
Where hope of salvation struggles against fear of death
The *tenor* voice of Hope
Drowning the fear in *alto*
and the voice of Christ sung by a *bass*
Eternity and you *word of thunder*
How can one live
A whole lifetime
Without some day falling in love
With such divinely beautiful musical dialogue?

There was a time I dreamt every night
Without fault
of immortal ladies
(In my world we believed that such ladies existed).
I dreamt of their kindness
Their sweet smile
and diaphanous long, long robes
Trailing behind them.

Their celestial beauty
forbade any desire
and inspired fear.

Yet, they were kind and sweet, and their nearness
created eternity of ecstasy.

There was a time when I fell in love with books
The older, the better.
My father and I competed to see
who finished first a whole library.
Now my father is gone
and the library is gone
The books remain in me
In each book , lives the soul of the man
or woman
who wrote it
and who hoped that their book would be read by many.
I answered the hope
and found in it moments of wonder.

There was a time when I fell in love with silence
it is true that after years of silence
one craves for the voice of others!
But for a long time silence
was all I hungered for,
wrapped in fierce rejection
Of any intrusion
Into the stream of my thought

There was a time …

DEATH

I have seen death up-close:
That afternoon he was riding his bicycle
with his young students
when a sudden gust of violent wind
enveloped them.
A heavy branch from a tall tree by the side of the road
was broken
and crashed and hit my friend on the neck.
People told us that he had gone safely away
but he turned his bike around and went back
when he heard the crash
perhaps to save his students.
But his students were all safe
while he was brought to the hospital.

We sat looking religiously
at our friend with a broken neck.
He breathed with a gurgling sound
as we -- young as we were -- knew it was the death-rattle.
that lasted for many hours,
Then, *fortunately*, the death-rattle ended.

*

I have seen death up-close:
A child running across the street
I child from the countryside
He was running after his dad
who had crossed safely to the other side,
and now looked back in horror.
The child was run over by a heavy truck
in the busy street.

The child emerged
from under the truck
holding his spilled entrails.

He fixed his dimmed eyes on his father
as if to say:
"Dad! Help me. I know you can!"
But his father was no miracle worker!
Fortunately,
The child died within a minute.
*

I have seen death up-close:
A young man carrying a child on his back
was running in the rice paddy.
Like us, he was a civilian running away from the war.
But soldiers kept firing down from the fortress walls
the same walls that our forefathers built
to protect our city.

They kept firing from the fortress walls
on us, erratically:
He screamed all a sudden:
"I am hit!"
We surrounded him
in the face of mortal danger.
We led him to the rice-paddy dyke
there he said softly:
"Take good care of the little girl".
She was not even related to him
just a little girl, lost in the war.
He died a few minutes later.
we had to move on
we left him on the levee
but we took the little girl.

Someone started carrying her on his back.
Fortunately the soldiers stopped shooting
from the fortress walls.
*

I have seen death up-close:

He breathed softly
we were happy that he breathed on,
even though it was labored breathing
We surrounded his bed
but love could not drive death away
that much we knew.
We looked at him
wondering how
wondering when
then our mind went blank.
It had been days since
the agony started
Nothing we could do.
And that day like the other days
we prayed and exhausted
all the prayers we knew by heart.
*

My sister made a remark
we turned around and looked at her just one second,
When our eyes went back to my father
he obviously had stopped breathing.
Fortunately he died in peace, my sister said,
Though the crying and sobbing
started soon after that.

O yes, I have seen death up-close!

SERENITY LAKE

A blue-tailed damselfly
flies across the expanse of Serenity Lake.
She seems oblivious
of two golden whistlers
perched on low-hanging branches
watching her with hungry, greedy eyes.

There were two wooden bridges
a long time ago
that linked the East and West Lake isles to the main road
that cut that hidden paradise in two.
The bridge to the Westlake Isle is no longer there.

With passing years and without repair
only rotting black wooden piles
remain in the middle of the lakes
wooden arms raised as if imploring
an unknown God.

Wooden piles
that support nothing except
an occasional bright green kingfisher
or a studious common tern.

As a child I came here almost on a daily basis
and ran past the wooden bridge
to the little isle on West Lake
Where earlier a rowdy and recalcitrant Child-Emperor,
it was said,
was forced to live in a little pavilion
in absolute isolation
until he learned to accept discipline.

When he did – only he was judge--
he only had to say to the Imperial Regents
that he had repented.
The legend goes on,
the whole Imperial Court
in their ceremonial dress
Came and knelt down in front of him
then got up, straightened their ceremonial dress
and accompanied him to the sounds of music
back to his golden palace.

I came there often as a child
pensive and sad
looking at the red and white lotus blossoms
their long and slender light green stems put them
high above a sea of jade green leaves.

I came there and sat
looking at kingfishers and common terns
that dived silently into the
Lake and came out with a large fish
in their inapt beaks.

We loved the walled garden
That included the lotus lakes,
and the man-made mountains on East Lake
(the bridge linking it to the main road still is standing)
where reclined feverish lovers
on man-made rocks.

Many said that in the rocky mountains on East Lake Isle
they saw ghosts in the moonlight.

I believe the ghosts were
Lovers who draped themselves in white sheets
To scare away prying intruders.

The sandy road that ran at the foot of the wall
espousing its contour
was also the favorite path
that tarrying couples of lovers
inebriated with the fragrance of lotus blossoms,
used to trod on,
at night
In the darkness or in the moonlight.
So inebriated,
And so full of desire
they seemed unable to find the garden exit
until the next morning.

My heart yearns for this hidden paradise
where my young dreams were born,
This place full of legends
This jewel of the Imperial City:
"Serenity Lake".

BALCONIES

I have stood on many balconies
looking out to the calm blue sea
or green mountains that climb up the far horizon.

I have stood on balconies
and looked down on the streets below
where the crowds of humans seem to know
where they must go
showing they have accepted their fate.

I have stood on the top of mountains
looking out at empty expanses
of sky and earth.

I have stood at the bow of tall ships
contemplating the heavy hulls cutting through giant waves
thinking fragility
of life, love, and friendship
and temptations of self-annihilation.

Someday on the balcony of heaven
I will stand, looking down on earth
loving humanity and its fragility
its labor and concerns
its fears and its hope.

I will love the men and women
who struggle
while knowing
that life should not be a battlefield
and that someday their struggle will stop
allowing them to stand on the balcony of heaven

looking down on earth
loving the men and women who are still struggling
who are still hoping when only despair
and surrender are the only
logical options for their fate.

I have stood on so many balconies
mountaintops and large ships' bows
where I have seen everything
changes
and acquires new meanings.

HOPE

Hope is at the core of our being,
destroy hope, you destroy life
and perhaps more than life itself.

Hope is more precious than faith
For without faith you still are human
without hope you have no map to find the direction
to eternity
and life becomes absurd,
and the world a vast prison where you listen to
an incomprehensible life sentence
read and reread laboriously on loudspeakers
by illiterate and invisible wardens
who mangle its every word.

I know there is an escape!
But it would be cowardice
if we choose to take it.

Without hope
we move in a cold twilight
cursing the gods
who gave us life.

Without hope
most human relationships stop,
dialogues end or never start
words are empty promises
love freezes right in the heart.

I have crossed immense deserts
encouraged as I was by hope.

Without it
there would be no caravans moving
in all Sahara.

Without hope no ship would sail on the seven seas
no bird would fly south after the summer
or north in springtime.

Without hope
no flower would blossom
even for a short hour
(like the glorious glory-mornings
under my window).

Without hope no dream could be built
And reality is reduced
To immense mounds
of grey ashes.

DESERT

"After this high dune we will see the city
shining in the distance", he said.
But after that dune there was another dune
and other dunes after that one.
No city in the distance
No oasis
No fresh breeze!
This is a deadly desert
men cross it in caravans
with heavily burdened dromedaries.
Men cross it calling out to each other
in Saharan Arabic.
We are walking in that desert, my friend,
when exhausted you will see mirages
of blue water in the distance
you will run to the shimmering water edge
then fall in despair to your knees
as water turns into sand again.
This desert is vast
here and there white skulls of past adventurers gleam
under the unforgiven sun.
The only recent travelers here are horned desert vipers
And spitting cobras.
So walk on, travelers
do not nurse vain hopes!
Your survival is in the hand of the Almighty,
just walk on
and if exhaustion, thirst and despair
descend on your agony
know that other travelers
stronger, better supplied, with better maps
have closed their eyes at death's door
and felt sweet resignation wrap its wings
Around them and taken them to where mirages become realities.

HOMEWARD

Like you, I am homeward bound
after a long pilgrimage
to alien places and unfamiliar shrines.
Like you, I long for sweet evenings
enjoying the reassuring flames
dancing in the fireplace

Like you, I have followed Ulysses' route
landing where monsters and cyclops live
made prisoner here and there
shipwrecked a dozen times.
Now like you I long for a long rest
in my sweet home,

In the arms of my sweet wife
Who has waited for me in silence
Muttering at times idle prayers.

I long for the final rest
That knows how to bury all memories of my adventures.
I long for the final rest
When my eyes close
And never reopen ever again.

MOONLIGHT

Walking with you in this ylang-ylang scented garden
I understand
why we want the night to last
forever!

The drooping yellow flowers
almost white under the moonlight
exhale memories and regrets
as we walk dreamily hand in hand
while the ylang-ylang scented garden
listen to the wilderness beyond the fences.
*

We wanted the night to last forever
in the ylang-ylang scented garden.
But the wilderness
even when bathed in moonlight
waited outside the garden
ready to pounce on us.

Do you remember that night
when time marked a pause?
But then it was urged
by the insensate world
to hurry on.

Yet, we still have the memory
of that moonlit night,
(and no regret)
When we walked in that paradise
Hand in hand
Breathing in the intoxicating
Scent of ylang-ylang.

THE OLD BUDDHIST MONK

He walked slowly up to the mountaintop
the will was stronger than the body.
His pagoda was midway to the top
there he spent half the day
and many hours far into the night.

But every morning before sunrise
he walked up the winding path
created by his unsteady steps
to where he could see all the plain
as the sea of mist
faded in the morning light.

Ten years already, he never talked.
Only his withered hand told his only novice
what he wanted.
The hands moved slowly
whenever they talked
And even that was rarely, extremely rare!

When young I went to see the old monk on a monthly basis.

I brushed aside his only novice
who was afraid I troubled his master's peace of mind
and delayed – by so doing -- his master's attaining
Buddhahood.

The old monk never said a word
never spoke to me with his withered hand
I read his eerie messages
from his frozen body
and his unmoved lips

We sat opposite
his mind flowed into mine
I learned from him a thousand things
Sitting opposite
knowing that he would never open his eyes
or move his lips.

Since those years I was more his disciple
than his only disciple in the pagoda
who took care of him day and night
and who cremated the remains the old monk
when the final change took place
and gathered his holy relics or pearly ringsels.

I was not there when the old monk died
I did not attend his cremation
I did not gathered his holy relics
But his spiritual *sarira*
have remained within me over ten thousand days after his passing
and very probably to the day I die.

MEDITATIONS

A prolonged focus on a simple word
or a barely emerging idea
a long silence after a short prayer
a world of visions that come more from the mind
than reality.
Does it mean
You meditate?
When your hand stretches over the Cross and a skull
While you kneel and lower your head?
Do you meditate?
When you watch
A lengthy pause in the midst of rapid fire sword dance?
Do you meditate?
In your lonely journey into nothingness?
Anybody, please come up with a valid definition
of meditations!
Those who know they are standing on a bridge
to nowhere
and those who agonize in unending solitary confinement,
trying to lure their laconic wardens
Into a short exchange,
understand more than most of us
the worth of meditations!
Have you stood on a bridge to nowhere?
Have you been years after years in solitary confinement?
Have you prayed all winter to a silent god?
Have you stared uncomprehending all summer
at cabalistic signs on the walls of an ancient cave ?
If you haven't,
don't you talk to me
about meditations!

MEMORIES

Streams of memories
flow where no dams could be constructed.
Oh, do not try!
They will breach on the first onslaught.

Painful memories that would make angels weep
searing memories made of guilt and shame,
beloved eyes that had closed
flowers that had withered
bodies that had dissolved
dreams that had bred nightmares
order that had turned into chaos!

Are they the only remnants of time past?
Oh, I still remember glorious sunsets
observed from my old village
and the calming peace
of rustic dawns.
I still remember my childhood companions
dashing and jumping on the grass near the riverbank.

I still remember how we hunted together
treasures that had never existed.
How we laughed
when we sat around a campfire
ash-roasting our sweet potatoes
and our chestnuts!

I remember how we grew up
each one went his or her way
pursuing careers or glory
never to return
to the humble village,
our birthplace!

So good memories may turn
into regrets and despair.
Time is unforgiving
we have learned that, growing up
we watch the streams of our memories
with a little melancholy
but not dejection.

There is no desolation here,
just a little pensiveness.
and with a little chance,
we will survive our memories!

HATRED

I would not hate him if his ears were not *that* pointy!
and his nose *that* crooked,
I would not hate him if the mere thought of him
did not make my nights sleepless!
Well, if my nights are sleepless
I make sure his waking hours
worse than hellish!

We were friends sometime in the past.
I cannot figure out why!
not a close friend, mind you!
But even in those days my feelers were out!
I vaguely suspected him
of being a two-faced psychopath
and a slight-handed cheater
in our penny ante poker games.

I suspect his sphinx of a wife
treacherous and merciless and ravenous
has over the years killed and eaten
all the little traits that was good in him
leaving him a pathetic monster
that trembles under her lion haunches.

No, I am not consumed with hatred,
as my confessor would like me to acknowledge
before he grants me absolution!

I left the confessional *unforgiven*
Adding the name of the silly priest
To the list of my enemies
Feeling relieved
More than at any time in my recent past!
Nursing my hatred I continue my pilgrimage
to uncertain heavens.

THE OLD CHURCH

Thirty years ago
The bishop came and inaugurated
The St Jude's church
unaware perhaps that the saint
is the patron saint of lost causes!

It was a long time ago
the crowd of believers that day
could not find enough seats inside;
and there were throngs outside
claiming they were believers too.

For hours the church bells
rang as if they were announcing total victory
at the end of a World War!
They rang before the bishop's arrival,
during the inauguration ceremony
and many times during the Mass
they rang as the Bishop emerged from the church
with the believers who had found seats inside.

The joy remained with the little parish
and for many years there were enough people
who came dutifully: all finding seats
inside the church,
On Sundays and Holy days of obligation.

Ten years ago,
Only a few people showed up for Sundays
And most days of obligations.
and couples dutifully married in the church.

Five years ago,
The exodus continued unabated
and the priest from another parish
came to say Mass only when he could.

He finally reported that such trips
Were no longer worth it
as the collection dwindled
To a few coins
Slipped furtively into the collection basket
By a few visibly invalid widows.

Three years ago
The church was auctioned off
There were no conditions in the bill of sale .
the church could be used for any purpose
apparently.

Recently,
The bell tower was decapitated
the church vaulted ceilings
allowed the new owner to transform
St. Jude's into a two-floor hotel

A month ago,
We came and rented a room on the upper floor
We could not sleep as in the darkness
we felt distinctly the light touch of angels 'wings
All night long!
(to those who ask :
"why do you object to be touched by angels' wings
My answer is, I don't mind if
That happens after I am dead;
But while I'm alive
There's no fun for me to be reminded
of another world)
Travelers beware!
Even if recommended by trivago or airbnb
never book a room at St. Jude Hotel,
as St Jude is the saint patron of lost causes
and St Jude Hotel
with its decapitated bell-tower
is at night haunted by angry angels.

THE PAGODA

The pagoda is not where you meet Buddha
It's simply where you meet yourself.
Of course there are large statues of Shakyamuni
and there are giant bronze incense burners
and kneeling worshippers
But the worshippers went to the wrong place!
They seem not to know
Buddha doesn't need worshippers.
Here is only a place
Where you meet yourself.
I often come to pagodas
And sit where I can hear the chanting of Buddhist prayers.
The monotonous and endless chants
of the believers
who feel the need of breaking
the cycle of death and reincarnation
who want to escape from earthly desires causing
Rebirths.
I often come and sit in pagodas
learning about nothingness.
Not longing for Nirvana
my sense fully awake
as I listen to the chants
of familiar mantras.
My mind doesn't look for the state
of Bodhisattva.
It is here I learn
To meditate
On human fate
And compassion.
I often come and sit in a pagoda
And feel sustained by millions of believers
Who pray day and night for the ultimate escape
From suffering and human fate.

WORDS

Words betray when we need them most:
Words to confess our first love,
Words to leave the last wish,
Words that contain the weight of our life,
Words formulated on our lips
But not born into sounds.
Words are all we have
They were born with our race
They are the mark of our culture
They are transmitted from age to age
From generation to generation
They multiply and expand
Forming horizons, forming oceans

We carry them in our bosom
Knowing how precious they are
Have been and will always be

They say silence is gold!
What a joke!
We cannot live in a world of silence:
Silence entombs our bodies,
Freezes our thought,
Negates our will
And makes a mockery of all our dreams.

Granted silence is the pre-thought world
And silence may be the sign of deep love
It also may be the floor of deep hatred

Give me back the words, please
Let me live with the words
That have created my being
Within the being of my nation
And my race.

INSPIRATION

It only takes little noise
to make a bird fly away.
It only takes a teardrop to move a merciful god
(so they said).
It only takes an original impulse to make a planet
Rotate upon itself and circle around a star.
It only takes a word
To start a poem or a thousand-page novel.
It only takes a little love to give happiness
To two lonely souls
It only takes an idea
To revolutionize the world
It only takes a good book
To transform a thousand lives
It only takes a penny to start
The carrier of a fortune-builder
It only takes a blade of grass
To create a great poet.
It only takes the glimpse of a dream
To start an empire.
It only takes a flitting vision of beauty
To make the world endurable.
It only takes a drop of water
Followed by other drops of water
To make a river.
It only takes a stumble
To cause a fall of a thousand feet.
It only takes a little match
To start a forest fire.
It only takes a little mistake
To ruin an entire kingdom
It only takes a whisper to ruin a good reputation…

HER SADNESS

The sea is immense
Immense is her sadness
The sea ebbs and flows
Her sorrow knows no ebbing

THERE COMES A TIME
In memory of Tom Barnes,
USMC, USAID, USDS, UNHCR, ICMC, my friend.

There comes a time when pain wouldn't go away,
When tired eyes barely see the light of day,
When colors fade and a jungle drum beats like the heavy
Hammer striking at the brain and the heart,
And when the faces of loved ones became hazy,
Then, it is time to go, my dear
To where the voice of pine trees is fresh and clear,
Back to that beach with white rocks and emerald water,
Back to the time where regrets were sweet and dreams mattered.
For a long time, we, your friends, will not forget
The nightly screams of seagulls over Leman Lake;
For a long time we will, for old time's sake,
Stroll the beaches where night and day reach out until they meet
One minute, in glorious twilight
Then yield the place to total darkness.
For the longest time, we will visit the sites of your pilgrimages
Where multitudes were slaughtered while we stood helpless
And watched the corruption of the monsters on stages
Swallowing entire nations.
For the longest time we will witness
Like you did, the long march of survivors winding in the wilderness
Finding no asylum or mercy anywhere.
Yet, there were places that had given you strength,
There were moments that had made you shake with happiness.
We will go back there too and visit at length and
treasure the short moments where we and you had found blessedness.
You the yellow- haired boy laughing in the field of golden wheat,
You the young man crouched in the trench strewn with body parts,
You the quiet observer of man's ambitions, envy and greed
You, the helpless helper with a broken heart
Rest, dear friend, until again we will all meet
To chat and laugh, and remember under distant stars.

WAITING FOR DAWN

Tears rolled down on the pillow
The blanket did not cover the darkness
Inside the room and ourside the windows
She lay waiting for dawn
That might never come back

Night after night the darkness stayed longer
Over her heart and her world
Like a tepid membrane
That never retracted before the long-awaited dawn.

Then one night, she shriked and tore the darkness
She had finally found the strength to shrike
And the darkness was gone.

She stood up before dawn
Wondreing why she had not done so earlier
Why she had laid in the darkness
Unable to move.
When dawn came she was ready
She received it with outreached arms
Embracing that old friend
Who had eluded her night after night

She ran down the stairs into he rose garden
The fragrance of the roses
Envoloped her
And she fell back into the darkness
The darkness that had defeated the sunlight

Now she lay in her bed
Surrounded by the whisper of darkness
That wrapped her in its soft, wet and dark fingers
And made sure that she would not see dawn ever again.

THE EMPTY CHURCH

It is the time of plague
The church's doors are open
But nobody comes in
No whispered prayer
Except that of stray dry leaves
Blowed in by gusts of cold wind

The dry leaves seem to aim for the altar
But are stranded here and there on the cold floor
Of the empty church
The dry leaves whisper no prayer

The priest is not in the empty church
He is busy working on his homily that he
Never delivers
And may end up sent out in an email
To cowered parishioners

Some of them watch Mass online
Until, at last they even drop that
As TV Mass is no Mass at all
And parishioners are no longer the faithful
But only prisoners of a virus.

Prisoners of fear
They have forgotten there is the God of love
They have forgotten the burning thirst
Of the Body and Blood of the One
Who died, abandoned on the Cross.

Fear makes the empty church
Farther and farther from them
Until it disappears, along with the priest,
buried in the plague,
The great equalizer.

THE QUARANTINED LADY

She was quarantined in her apartment
For months she only saw people on her television
And talked to people on her I-phone.
She was alone
In her vast apartment
Skipping meals and sleep
Waiting the verdict
That might come someday.
She was not afraid
But feeling no fear when surrounded by death
Was worse than being scared
The absence of fear
Was worse when combined with the indifferent embrace of death.
She kept a diary
But quite a few days went without an entry
She tried to read books
But never finished one.
She walked back and forth in her apartment
Knowing that in the neighboring buildings
People were carried out
And never came back
The sun never showed up
The sky looked indifferent
Somehow, she thought someday electricity would be cut off
She thought they would come and cut off her water too.
The city, as far as she could see
Was deserted, except for a couple of stray dogs
And a couple of oversized rats
She had lost her sense of time
And could not know what month she was in
Not that she cared to know.
Then, one day they came and carried her out
And she never came back.

About the Author

About ANDRÉ NGUYN VAN CHÂU

Andre Nguyen Van Chau was born in the Citadel of Hue, the old capital of Imperial Vietnam. He grew up with classmates who have become known writers, poets, composers and painters.

After obtaining a doctorate degree in the humanities at the Sorbonne, Paris, he taught English and creative writing at various universities in Viet Nam for twelve years.

In 1975 he began twenty-five years of work for migrants and refugees around the world, ten of which were spent at the head of the International Catholic Migrations Commissions with 84 national affiliates and with headquarters in Geneva, Switzerland.

He has traveled and worked in over 90 countries.

Back to the United States after Geneva he was for ten years the Director, Language and Accent Training at ACS, then Xerox before retiring in Austin, Texas and beginning a new career as a full-time writer.

One of his published works, *The Miracle of Hope,* has been translated into nine different languages.

The New Vietnamese-English Dictionary, on which he spent an inordinate number of hours in the last twenty years, was finally published in 2014.

He and his wife, Sagrario, have four children: Andrew, married to Jodie Scales, Boi-Lan, married to Rodolphe Lemoine, Michael, married to Rachel La Fleur and Xavier. They have seven grandchildren: Katelyn, Géraldine, Alix, Drew, Noah, Isabelle and Luke.

Other Books By This Author:

The New Vietnamese - English Dictionary

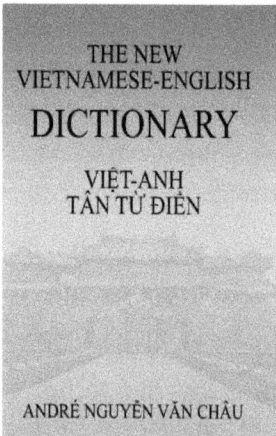

THE NEW
VIETNAMESE-ENGLISH
DICTIONARY

VIỆT-ANH
TÂN TỪ ĐIỂN

ANDRÉ NGUYỄN VĂN CHÂU

This is an advanced Vietnamese dictionary with English definitions, compiled with the enrichment of the Vietnamese language in mind.

This dictionary lists words and expressions used by Vietnamese throughout the ages. It shows local and ethnic dialectal words and phrases and promotes the understanding of the Vietnamese culture past and present.

Over 1170 pages! – The most comprehensive collection to date.

A Lifetime in the Eye of the Storm

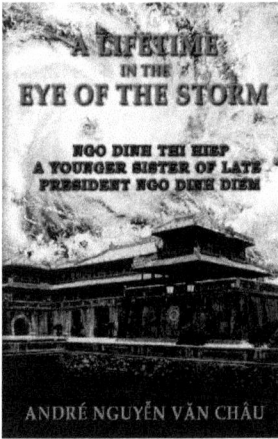

History is colored by the nation that is recording it. In America, the Vietnam War was chronicled in the newspapers and on television. The heart breaking stories we heard were always about the war from the American viewpoint. When we are able to view historical events from perspectives other than our own, we begin to understand that the important thing isn't winning or losing, but learning and understanding.

Hiep lived her life, from earliest childhood, at the center of the war. This is her story of love and loss, triumph and tragedy. It is the story of all women who have lived through a war, with only their steadfast love, hope and faith in God to give them the strength to go on living.

"A moving account of the Ngo Dinh family's determination to live and work for the freedom of their beloved country."

Journeys into Darkness and Light

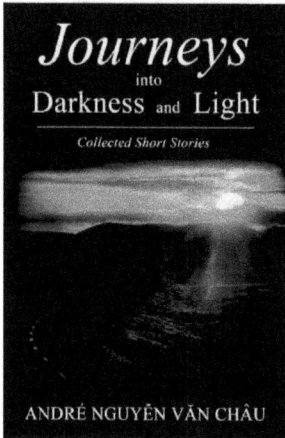

Born in Vietnam in 1935, André Nguyễn Văn Châu grew up in the midst of wars; enduring intense emotions ranging between hopes and disappointment to joys and sorrows. Many of the stories he penned in 'Journeys into Darkness and Light' set tragic characters against terrible odds. Most of them triumphed over their despair, or accepted their demise with superhuman courage.

Later in his life the author lived and worked in scores of countries where men and women from different parts of the world, especially in Africa, shared the same joys and sorrows with their Vietnamese contemporaries. He spoke of them and shared their stories with the same tenderness, complicity, and emotional intensity.

The brevity of these stories considerably enhances the general theme. It highlights the loneliness, alienation, terror in the face of the passing of time and death, in the characters, and also their surging moments of happiness and hope.

Night and Day

Night *and* Day

Collected Short Stories

ANDRÉ NGUYỄN VĂN CHÂU

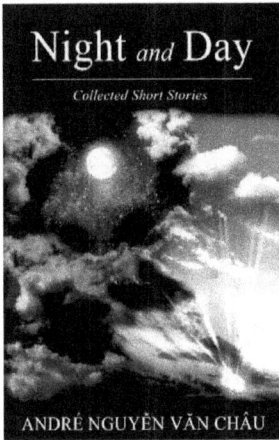

After successfully launching *"Journeys into Darkness and Light"* a collection of short stories in April 2015, André Nguyễn Văn Châu penned three longer fiction works included within *"Night and Day"*.

These multi-faceted stories follow the characters into dark despair so they can overcome their ordeals in order to start believing again. The point of departure might be sin, crime, or a moment of weakness, but the end-game is redemption, a violent confrontation with fate, and enlightenment.

Always depicting the men and women of his stories with tenderness and respect Van Chau illustrates their pain, defeat, triumph, and joy as if these emotions were his own. When the final confrontation leads to the possibility of redemption or an invitation to holiness, you know you will walk away from these stories with a new perspective.

The Miracle of Hope

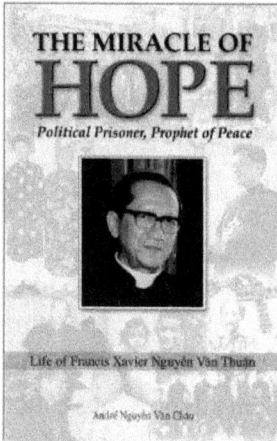

Known to many Catholics through his writings (Testimony of Hope; The Road of Hope), Vietnam's late Cardinal Francis Xavier Nguyen Van Thuan's amazing story is told by a former fellow seminarian who knew him from the time the cardinal was 18. Chau initially declined the cardinal's request to write about his life, but in 1999, reluctantly agreed, finishing the book just a few months before the cardinal died in 2002. Chau has meticulously chronicled Cardinal Thuan's life and that of his prominent family, which paid dearly for its involvement in the quest for Vietnam's independence. To help the reader navigate through a complex cast of characters, Chau has included a glossary and an explanation of Vietnamese personal names. He portrays Cardinal Thuan as a humble man who gladly would have served as a rural pastor, but was marked for leadership in the church early on. Even as he prepared for this role studying in Europe, Cardinal Thuan had a premonition that he would suffer martyrdom, and indeed, after being named coadjutor archbishop of Saigon in 1975, he was arrested by Communist authorities. Thuan subsequently spent 13 years in prison, which shaped his spirituality and leadership. ~ *Publishers Weekly*

www.ingramcontent.com/pod-product-compliance
Lightning Source LLC
Chambersburg PA
CBHW070831100426
42813CB00003B/573